Lofts

Lofts

Living and working spaces

Author Francisco Asensio Cerver

Editorial Director Paco Asensio

Project co-ordinator Ivan Bercedo / Itziar Sen

Design & Layout Mireia Casanovas Soley

Text The designers

Translation David Buss

Proofreading Harry Paul

Copy editing Michael Webb

First published in 1999 by **arco**
for Hearst Books International
1350 Avenue of the Americas
New York, NY 10019

Distributed in the U.S. and
Canada by
Watson-Guptill Publications
1515 Broadway
New York, NY 10036

Distributed throughout the rest
of the world by
Hearst Books International
1350 Avenue of the Americas
New York, NY 10019

2001 © Francisco Asensio Cerver

Printed in Spain
B2C

Legend has it that around the turn of the 20th century, all real painters lived in tiny garrets under the eaves of the Paris skyline, either paying minuscule rents or trying to avoid creditors. This, it is sometimes said, led to their paintings being on the small side, and if we look at the works of painters such as Paul Klee, Van Gogh, or Juan Gris, the idea might seem to stand up to analysis. At the same time, one look at a painting by Pollock, Motherwell, or Schnabel is enough to tell us that such a painting has probably not been created in a garret—either in Paris or elsewhere.

Although much has been written about the influence wrought on the history of art by chemical changes, the composition of paints, or even the use of one type of bristle or another, the repercussions that an artist's studio could have on his or her work have not often been considered.

The main transformation in painting during the second half of the 20th century has been the change of scale, and much of this transformation may indeed have been due to the artists' shift in residence from attics and other small studios to spaces formerly used as factories or warehouses. To paint a 150-square-foot canvas, a large studio is unavoidably necessary.

Mentioning artists in a book about lofts is appropriate, since artists were the first to see the advantages of taking old industrial premises and converting them into studios and dwellings. Perhaps Andy Warhol, with his notorious "factory," is the most famous example, but many urban-based artists of our time have also chosen this type of space in which to live and work. Even today, after the loft has ceased to be the exclusive prerogative of the artist and has become an acceptable, alternative form of housing, a large percentage of those living in these spaces are painters, photographers, architects, publicists, and other sorts of creative, or design and media-oriented professionals.

A driving force behind the loft phenomenon is the gradual abandonment of old industrial buildings by

companies looking for newer and better equipped premises. The result is that lofts are not to be found in all districts of a city, but only in those with an industrial past, such as Clerkenwell, Poblenou, or Soho. As competitive pressures drive industries to abandon their original homes, new activities for which the spaces are more than adequate are quickly replacing them.

The loft represents both the unconventional life of the artist who integrates home and work in one space and also an industrial tradition evident in the nature of the buildings themselves. The person who decides to live and work in a loft does so perhaps to some degree out of sympathy for the notions and feelings that the genre conjures up. Therefore, any conversion that is necessary should not substantially modify the space but instead equip it for new activities without changing its original look.

A simple definition of a loft might be as follows: a large space, almost always converted from nonresidential use, and usually having the structure and installations left exposed.

Although lofts are found in obsolete buildings that might seem less than ideal for a modern living space, precisely the opposite is true. Traditional houses are not always well suited to the changes brought about by communications technologies that allow more people to work out of their home. The distribution of space and functions, and the size of rooms, are based on fixed notions of bedroom, kitchen, living room, dining room, and so on. Adding work activities to this traditional blueprint requires a radical departure—not only more space is needed but more flexibility, as well.

Another factor is that the large nuclear family is rapidly becoming all but extinct. In large cities, such as New York or London, where the idea of the loft has been most thoroughly developed, one or two-person families are much more common than traditional families of four or more members. Smaller family units do not usually need the sort of privacy and partitioning found in a traditional home.

Lofts are large, flexible spaces that can evolve according to the needs of the people occupying them. This capacity to evolve will surely make lofts more prized in the future. A final point regarding the future of the loft is worthy of note: loft architecture is, in a sense, a significant form of recycling and reuse—critical concepts for the new century.

Living in a Loft

9

Changing Edges

K-Loft in New York City

George Ranalli

▶ This project is for the renovation of a 2,100-square-foot loft in the Chelsea section of New York City for two artists and their son. The building was constructed almost 90 years ago during the turn-of-the-century building boom in lower Manhattan. The interior has windows only in the front and rear. Because the loft is located on a lower floor of the building natural light is scarce. Therefore, the interior space had to be organized to take full advantage of any natural light and ventilation in the rooms as well as to fulfill the programmatic desires of the owners.

LOCATION: Chelsea section of New York City.

CLIENT: Jacque Metheny & Robert Kirschbaum.

AREA: 2,100 sq. ft. (195 sq. m)

COMPLETION DATE: 1996.

DESIGN TEAM: George Ranalli (principal & designer), John Butterworth (project architect), Stephania Rinaldi Kutscher, Nathaniel Worden (assistants).

CONSULTANTS: Robert Silman & Assoc. (structural), ACM Engineering (mechanical), Stephen Falk, Falk Assoc. (specifications), Joseph DiBernardo (lighting).

GENERAL CONTRACTOR: Lauda Construction.

PHOTOGRAPHY: Paul Warchol.

The existing space is a brick room with exposed brick bearing walls running the length of the space and a brick ceiling. The ceiling incorporates a series of vaults spanning steel sections from the front to the back of the loft. The existing room is a compelling space. A series of new forms are designed for the loft which accommodate the owner's program. These new shapes contain two new bedrooms, a new master bathroom, new kitchen, and a second bathroom. It was also the owner's intention that the feeling and quality of the original loft be maintained while designing the new spaces.

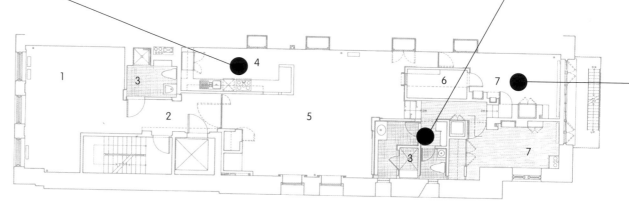

General floor plan.

1. Gallery
2. Hall
3. Bathroom
4. Kitchen
5. Living room
6. Store
7. Bedroom

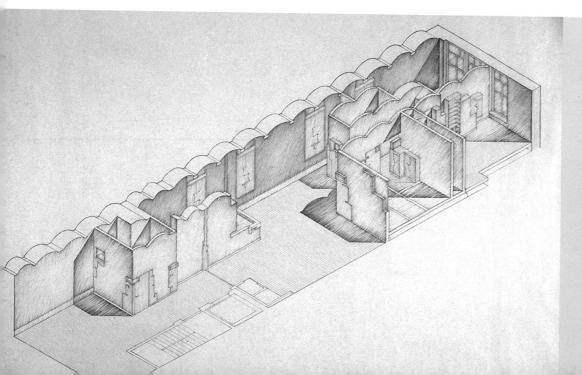

The project was designed and built out of highly finished materials to accentuate and contrast the rough container of the existing brick room.

Within the wooden panels is an intricate arrangement of screw fasteners. Alterations to the edges change the panel's profile. These design items have mainly to do with scale and surface treatment, emphasizing their overtly decorative aspirations.

The architectural design solution features a series of volumes sitting in the loft which allow the space of the room to remain unbroken. Each of the volumes takes a key position in the space so that it contains as well as produces space between the forms. Elements made of plaster include fixed translucent glass inserted in the blocks. These glass openings are meant to permit the passage of light and space from one room to another. The corners are protected with large panels of birch plywood cut in irregular profiles to help establish a secondary range of scale in the rooms. These panels are affixed to the plaster walls with a pattern of screw fasteners. All doors, lamps, cabinets, and other decorative objects are custom designed as part of the project.

Transparencies

Goldsborough Loft in London

AEM

▶ Glen Emrys and Pascal Madoc Jones, the two members of AEM, understood perfectly that the decision to convert a loft into a living space could not merely be an aesthetic choice because it denotes that the client has a certain attitude toward life and therefore requires that the architect comprehend this alternative point of view.

One of the factors coming into play is the love of open rooms, and the attraction felt for bare, unfurnished spaces. This commitment means, on one hand, that the architect must avoid dividing walls and must camouflage the storage spaces, and on the other hand, that the client must be able to overlap his or her activities in a single space. In this London loft the response to this choice has had excellent results, because the chromatic treatment given to the few pieces of furniture present, and the modeling of light through filters, are not only faithful to the commitment to refrain from altering the existing structure, but also manage to set free the potential lyricism of this type of space.

LOCATION: Clerkenwell, London EC1, United Kingdom.

CLIENT: Peter Goldsborough.

COMPLETION DATE: 1997.

DESIGN TEAM: Glen Emrys, Pascal Madoc Jones.

PHOTOGRAPHY: Alan Williams.

General floor plan.

1. Entrance
2. Kitchen
3. Living room
4. Stairs leding to the terrace
5. Store
6. Sauna
7. Bathroom
8. Bedroom

The architects' intention was to preserve the original open space without breaking it up into too many compartments. However, the privacy, both acoustic and visual, of the bedrooms had to be assured.

All facilities—the larder, kitchen, bath, and sauna—are located in the inside perimeter of the loft, occupying the niches and recesses of the wall separating the living space from the neighbor and from the stairwell.

An acid-etched glass screen and a clothes closet are used to demarcate the two bedrooms.

The location of the bathroom of the main bedroom makes it possible to turn a small space behind the entrance door into a hall.

The kitchen work top acts as an expressionist brushstroke which rounds off the color scheme of relaxed tones.

The existing metal structure was valued by the architects as an adaptable element that enriched the space.

Except for the most intimate activities, which are isolated in the bathroom and bedroom, nearly all everyday activities take place in the large, main open space. The magic of this room stems from its emptiness, and therefore furnishings have been kept to a minimum.

The acid-etched glass is not merely an architectural resort; it also has poetic value in its own right. The figures behind the glass lose definition. They become more spiritual and fragile, like the woman who levitates in the painting, or like the one who sits down to read in a chair made of air.

Variety Is the Spice of Life

Two Lofts in Gràcia

Joan Bach

▶ Although these two apartments have interiors designed by the same architect and are both located in the same building, they nevertheless represent two distinct visions of what the design for a loft can be. The different choices of materials, finishes, and even of furniture have given the spaces distinct characteristics.

In one of the lofts most of the structural elements, such as ceiling vaults, exterior wall, and trussed joints, have been left exposed, and a simple material—polished concrete—has been used for the floors. The loft has a decidedly industrial, even bleak, look. Two separate areas spread over the one-floor space: a large, square room, with one corner closed off to form an autonomous kitchen, and a surrounding strip of space which houses the bedrooms and bathrooms.

In contrast, the walls of the other loft are painted a shade of yellow, the flooring is parquet, the lighting is designed to give a warm light, and the furniture is new and functional. The space is divided into a large, split-level lounge with an open-plan kitchen and a lateral zone on three levels—the lower level containing the kitchen, stairs, and toilet; a mezzanine level housing the main bedroom with en suite bathroom and dressing room; and a third, independent level for children, with two bedrooms, a bathroom, and a playroom/study.

Location: Gràcia District, Barcelona.

Clients: Carles Portavella and Carlos Loverdos.

Date: 1998.

Design team: Joan Bach, Jordi Viladomiu, Ignasi Mas.

Consultants: Agesa (mechanical and electrical)

General contractor: Nicolás Olivares.

Photography: Jordi Miralles.

General plan.

1. Entrance
2. Kitchen
3. Utility room
4. Lounge
5. Bedroom
6. Dressing room
7. Bathroom
8. Toilet

Most of the furniture is second-hand, and its diversity gives the loft a heterogeneous look.

The partition walls do not reach the ceiling. This gives the loft a feeling of uninterrupted space. The pillar of exposed brick is not load-bearing—the building's structure is of metal—but rather contains the drainage pipes.

Lower floor.

Mezzanine.

Second floor.

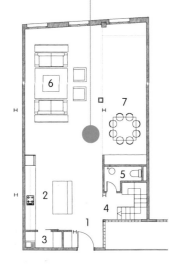

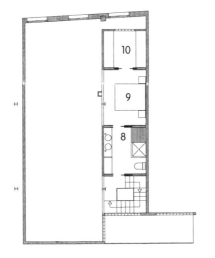

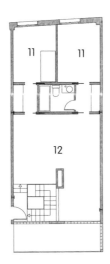

1. Entrance
2. Kitchen
3. Utility room
4. Stairs
5. Toilet
6. Lounge
7. Dining room
8. Bathroom
9. Main bedroom
10. Dressing room
11. Bedroom
12. Study

The architect achieves an interesting chromatic contrast between the surfaces painted in yellow and set against elements finished in a dark, burnt tone, such as beams, stairs, air ducts, kitchen, and even picture frames.

Although they are on different levels, the main bedroom and the lounge are connected visually.

The main bedroom is reached through the bathroom as though in a mosque, where ablutions are performed before entering a more sacred area.

House on a House

Penthouse in Vienna

Rüdiger Lainer

▶ A two-story penthouse conceived as a house built upon a house—a transparent entity replacing the existing pitched roof on one of the first reinforced-concrete apartment houses in the city.

The site is two minutes from the Stephansdom in the 1st district of Vienna's so-called holy central area and has a direct visual link to the cathedral. The façade of the existing building, built in 1911, imitates the historical character of the street despite the fact that the building was built recently. The penthouse therefore requires a thoroughly modern approach.

Two floor plates of exposed profile-metal sheets with a reinforced concrete deck supported by a steel frame create a flexible open space allowing multiple-room configurations.

The project is programmed to contain five entities, the combination and configurations of which allow the different zones to be used either as living or as office spaces, or as a combination of both. Furthermore, laminated glass is used in the central area as a roof to create a conceptual rift in the plan, thereby conveniently dividing the intervention into two distinct but interrelated zones. Interior space extends horizontally into the city and vertically toward the sky.

Hannes Schild

LOCATION: Seilergasse 16, Vienna, Austria.

CLIENT: Martin Schwanzer.

AREA: 5,800 sq. ft. (540 sq. m).

COMPLETION DATE: 1996.

PHOTOGRAPHY: Margherita Spiluttini (except as noted).

Modern glass technology combines with simple "industrial" structural elements.

The external skin of stainless steel uprights with clamped glass sheets fosters a link between the internal wooden floor and the external planted terraces, with unobstructed views of the dense urban fabric.

The project is programmed to contain five entities.

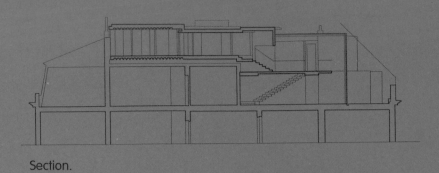

Section.

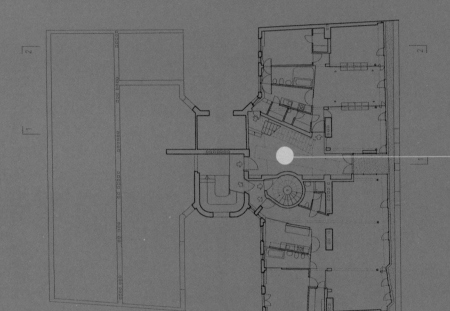

Lower level

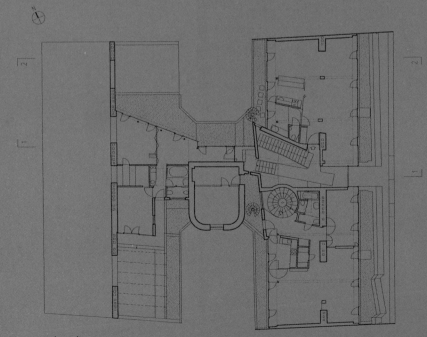

Upper level.

Hannes Schild

The building is two minutes away from the historic city centre of Vienna. It has excellent views over Saint Stephen's Cathedral. It is noteworthy that this project was granted planning permission despite the strict urban laws that control all reforms carried out to the Vienna city fabric.

The internal space extends horizontally towards the city and vertically towards the sky.

The service zones (bathrooms, kitchens, storage, and so on) are conceived as internally independent objects which help give order to the internal space. The materials, a combination of wood veneers and free-standing glass panels that give definition to the interior, create spatial transparency while still allowing for privacy.

The interior finishings (a combination of veneered wood and worked glass panels) are in tune with the diaphanous architecture, while at the same time respecting the privacy of the users.

Four Alternatives

Vapor Llull

Cirici & Bassó, Inés Rodríguez, Alfonso de Luna, Norman Cinamond, Carla Cirici

▶ Cristian Cirici and Carles Bassó have converted a former three-floor chemicals factory into housing, preserving the exterior brick walls with their handcrafted bays and the roof with its wooden trusses. Three blocks have been added for vertical communication, each consisting of a stairway and an exterior freight elevator, so that each of the eighteen apartments is independently accessible. The sophistication of the new elements contrasts with the traditional nature of the preserved structures and orange-and-blue facade.

Cirici & Bassó have left the inside of each apartment unfinished, with the idea that their plan would be carried further and completed by subsequent interior designers who would bring their own inspiration to each apartment. We have selected four of these interior designs—by Inés Rodríguez, Norman Cinamond, Alfonso de Luna and Clara Cirici—each with a distinctive design.

LOCATION: Llull 133, Barcelona.

CLIENT: Owners co-operative.

COMPLETION DATE: 1998.

COLLABORATORS: Jaume Sol (quantity surveyor).

GENERAL CONTRACTOR: UTE Audar-Coindur.

PHOTOGRAPHY: Rafael Vargas.

Transversal section.

42

10

5

2
1

Upper floor.

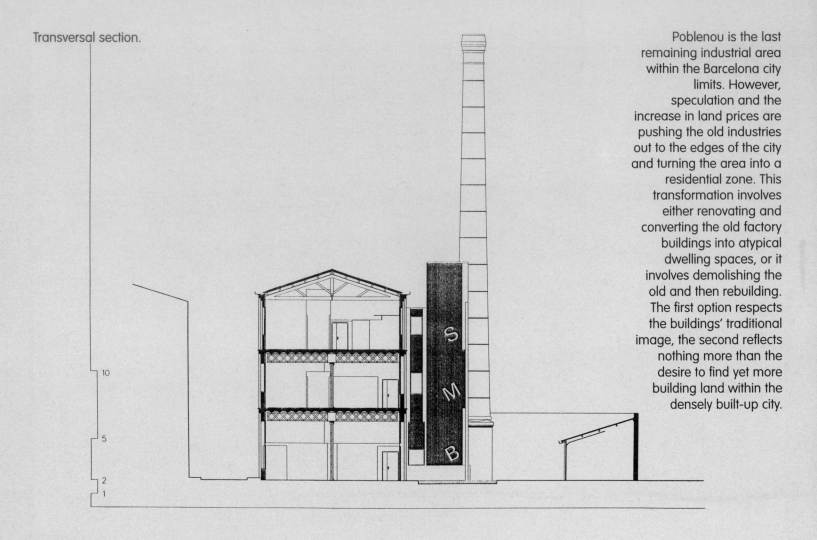

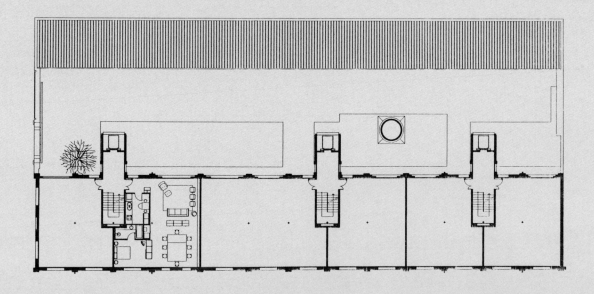

Poblenou is the last remaining industrial area within the Barcelona city limits. However, speculation and the increase in land prices are pushing the old industries out to the edges of the city and turning the area into a residential zone. This transformation involves either renovating and converting the old factory buildings into atypical dwelling spaces, or it involves demolishing the old and then rebuilding. The first option respects the buildings' traditional image, the second reflects nothing more than the desire to find yet more building land within the densely built-up city.

The use of large-scale letters and numbers in the façade and on the front doors of each apartment gives an industrial or graphic design appearance to the architecture.

The decision to leave the interiors unfinished and even unplastered has allowed greater flexibility and a wider range of designs.

Cirici & Bassó have preserved the old chimney of the steam boiler, isolating it as if it were a technological monument.

Inés Rodríguez has designed an austere attic in which the wooden roof trusses have a powerful presence.

The bedroom is contained in an alcove over the kitchen.

The flooring is of polished concrete and the walls are plastered and painted white. Scarcely any furniture can be seen and pictures are on the floor, leaning against the wall.

Norman Cinamond has opted for a densely furnished space dominated by reddish tones.

A counter separates the kitchen and the living room, acting as an informal dining area. The "Jamaica" model stools are by Pepe Cortés.

A picture by Antonio Saura hangs over the bed.

48

The extensive use of wood, the
flooring of tuff, the palms, and the
primitive sculptures give the
apartment designed by
Alfonso de Luna a misleadingly
tropical and decadent air.

Of the designs shown, **Carla Cirici**'s is the
one which least modifies the original space.

Thanks to a partially acid-washed glass door,
natural light reaches the entrance hall
from the kitchen.

Art & Humor

Sleeping in a Post Office

Orefelt Associates

▶ The Project is the conversion of an old postal service mail processing office into a residential building with an artist's paint studio. The brief was for two bedrooms, two bathrooms, living area and kitchen, paint studio, and a roof terrace. The obvious way of doing the layout would have been to put a mezzanine at the back for the bedrooms, kitchen, and bathrooms, with a double-height living room at the front. However, the actual plan is reversed. Stepping through the wooden entrance door one finds oneself in a hall between two free-standing boxes built into the space. A corridor and a staircase lead left. Beyond is a room with a terrazzo, which is a sky lit painter's workshop and studio. The living room and kitchen/dining area is at the top, also sky lit. The painter's studio is at the back for easier access. A stair between the kitchen and the dining area leads further up to the roof terrace that looks back down through the house.

LOCATION: 24 Hewer Street, London.

CLIENT: F. Larsson.

AREA: 2,900 sq. ft. (270 sq. m).

COMPLETION DATE: 1997.

DESIGN TEAM: Gunnar Orefelt, Knut Hovland.

CONSULTANTS: Orla Kelly & Michael Beagent (structural engineers); Applied Energy (services engineers); Roger Rawlinson Associates (quantity surveyor).

GENERAL CONTRACTOR: Day Building.

PHOTOGRAPHY: Alberto Ferrero.

The stairs, situated in the center of the house, constitute the spinal column of the dwelling.

The house has been thought out so that it can host large parties. This is why there is a visual connection between all the floors and the skylights from the terrace. The sixteen loudspeakers distributed around the house are another factor.

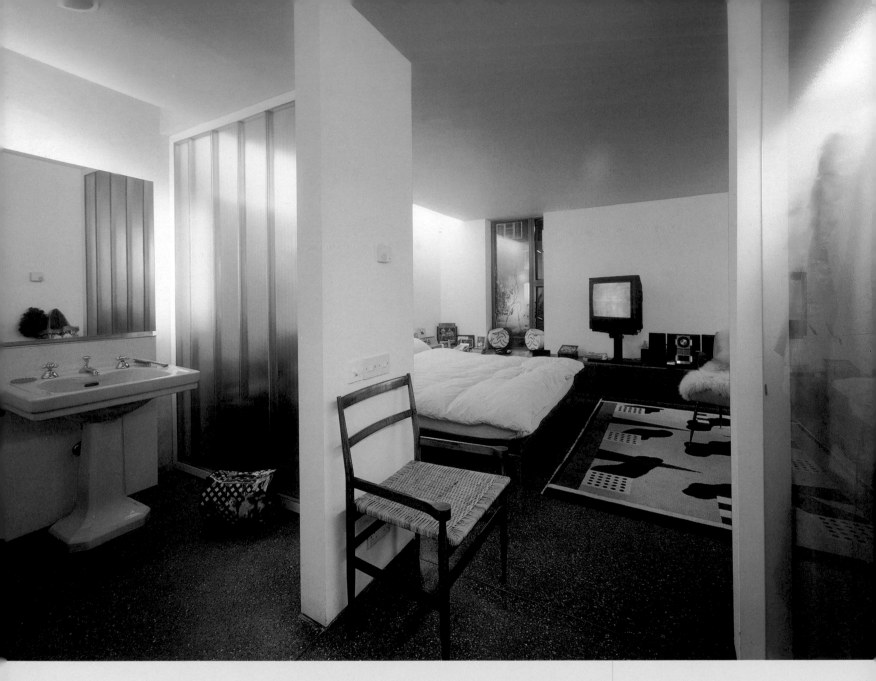

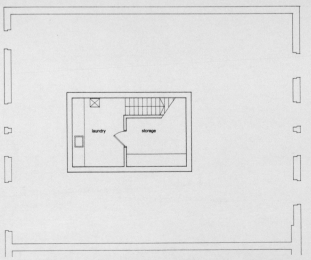

Basement.

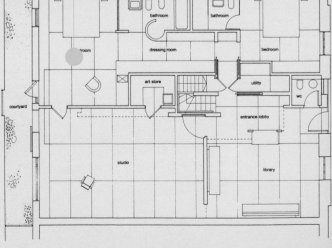

Ground floor.

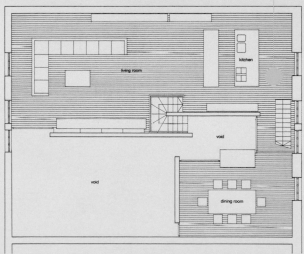

First floor.

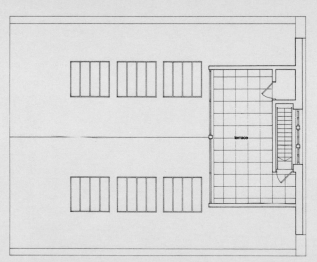

Terrace.

The interior is a bit like a Chinese puzzle; it constantly throws up new surprises, angles, and unexpected views.

The furniture and decoration chosen by the client is somewhat kitsch. The leopard-covered sofa, a rug decorated with Snow White and the seven dwarfs, a dog by Jeff Koons, and a large selection of plastic toys from a fast-food restaurant.

The house is designed for hosting parties. Sixteen speakers pipe music throughout the house.

Soho Lofts

Penthouses in Wardour Street

CZWG Architects

▶ The penthouses at Wardour Street grow out of the architecture below. Rather than a differentiated architectural treatment, they take on the primary form of the loft spaces below with their industrial materials and raw space and develop its expression more freely as the floors rise. Their are entirely new purpose built spaces. The primary structure is steel frame, which is kept fully exposed throughout lending the volumes a strong visual framework and rhythm. While the trumpet form of the internal lightwell results in that part of the frame being dramatically curved inside the space.

LOCATION: 10 Richmond Mews, London, United Kingdom.

CLIENT: Manhattan Loft Corporation Limited.

COST: £ 1,8 M

AREA: 14,348 sq-ft (1,333 m^2).

COMPLETION DATE: 1996.

DESIGN TEAM: Piers Gough, Nicholas Campbell, Rex Wilkinson (principals); Stephen Rigg, Jay Stuart, Luigi Beltrandi, James Corcoran, Sanjiv M. Gahil, Paul Jeffreys (associates).

CONSULTANTS: Envirotemp (service engineers); Vincent Grant Partnership (structural engineers); Leslie Clark & Partners (quantity surveyors); Allslade Makingstee (steelwork).

GENERAL CONTRACTOR: Higgs & Hill Southern Ltd.

PHOTOGRAPY: Chris Gascoigne.

The Penthouses don't only exploit the view. With their long slow curved silhouettes their are intended to add their own particular contribution to the amazing skyline.

The walls on the 5th floor have fully glazed runs of floor to ceiling window detailed in W20 section steel as the floors below. They open onto wide paved terraces facing east/west giving this floor a strong orientation in that direction. The sixth floor is orientated the other way with large north/south to give major views at right angles to those on the floors below, while the large terraces at this level command panoramic views across the roof tops of Soho.

The internal space at the upper level has the curved roof rising to a double height space supported on a rising series of steel portal frames. The windows onto the lightwell are continuous past the floor down to the 5th allowing the opportunity to open up further height with balconies or stairs.

Loft + Penthouse = ...

Oliver's Wharf

McDowell + Benedetti Architects

▶ Oliver's Wharf, a tea warehouse dating from the 1870s, was one of the first Docklands warehouses to be converted to residential use in the early 1970s. The penthouse apartment on the top two floors, with its extraordinary views across London, was the home of the architect who redeveloped the building. However, by the time the current owner purchased the apartment, it had been stripped out and left as a dilapidated shell.

The existing property was a 250-square-meter, double-height space with cast iron columns supporting massive oak trusses and a complex pitched roof. The architects' scheme completely remodeled the interior, introducing mezzanine platforms, a rooftop extension, two terraces, and extensive repair to the existing fabric. The finished apartment has an area of over 400 square meters, including terraces.

The layout of the apartment is centered on the kitchen at the main level, around which a sequence of spaces revolves: entrance hall, stair, gallery, sitting area centered around the fireplace, sitting area with views, and dining area. A small study/bedroom adjacent to the entrance has a fold-down bed and a shower/WC, and can be closed off for privacy.

At a high level within the main volume are two separate, open mezzanine platforms. The main bedroom occupies one platform and opens out to its own terrace. The other platform over the fireplace area is a small studio with a huge pivoting window overlooking the river.

LOCATION: London.

COMPLETION DATE: 1996.

AREA: 4,300 sq. ft. (400 sq. m)

COST: £450,000.

DESIGN TEAM: Jonathan McDowell, Renato Benedetti, Helen Berresford, Susan LeGood, Steve Perkins.

CONSULTANTS: Dewhurst MacFarlane and Partners (structural engineer); Fulcrum Consulting (mechanical and electrical engineer).

CONTRACTOR: Costfield; BLS Contracting.

PHOTOGRAPHY: Tim Soar.

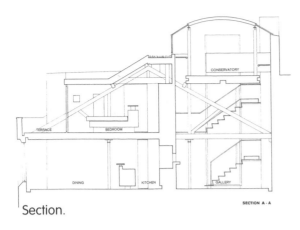

Section.

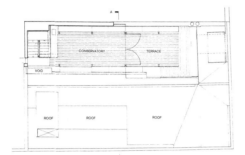

Terrace.

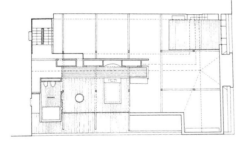

Upper level.

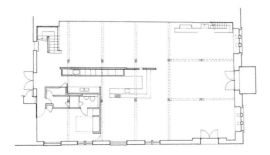

Lower level.

The new extension of roof level provides a lounge space opening on to a terrace with 360-degree views over London. Cast-glass seats supported on steel frames run along both sides of the roof room and out to the terrace, which has access to the gallery below.

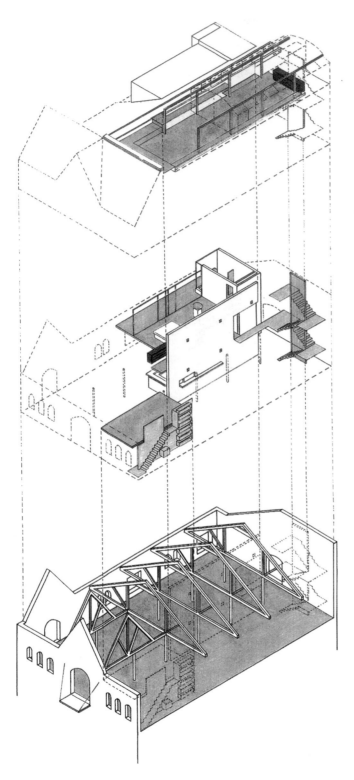

The new interventions act as focal objects to articulate the space and are made from simply detailed natural materials which contrast with the rough existing fabric.

The entrapped bubbles and slight texturing of the green, hand-cast glass, which was developed with Jeff Bell, has an appearance like that of melting ice.

The main spatial division within the open-plan volume was achieved by inserting a solid, three-story-high, 200-millimeter-thick limestone wall along the center of the space. The wall is backed with a layer of storage and services cupboards at kitchen and bedroom levels.

Unit 12

Loft in Clerkenwell

Circus Architects

▶ The loft was converted from two shell spaces in Clerkenwell, an area which is the focus for Soho-style loft spaces in London. The building itself was a print shop built in the 1930s and was converted to shell spaces for residential use by Manhattan Loft Corporation in the early 1990s. The concrete frame structure and huge metal-framed windows give the building an attractive industrial aesthetic which the developer enhanced with white painted plaster. MLC recommended Circus to the client, a family of four plus their dog. Circus had already completed two conversions in the building and subsequently has completed around fifty more loft apartments in London.

The elements inserted into the shell to order the space are curvilinear, contrasting with the rectilinear form of the existing structure. The feeling one has when moving from the closely placed, free-form, curvaceous elements of the lobby into the reception is intended to evoke the feeling of emerging from a narrow pass into a great canyon.

The major insertion was a mezzanine level. The initial idea was that no intervention or alteration would be made at any level above a meter of this mezzanine and that the raw shell would be exposed. This concept was later shelved, but the ceiling and double-height walls are minimally treated and retain their industrial aesthetic.

LOCATION: Unit 12, 1-10 Summer's Street, London.

CLIENT: Vaight family.

COMPLETION DATE: 1996.

DESIGN TEAM: Duncan Chapman (architect).

CONTRACTOR: James Riddell, Harley Cronyn.

PHOTOGRAPHY: Martin Levint (collage), Richard Glover.

The proje◀

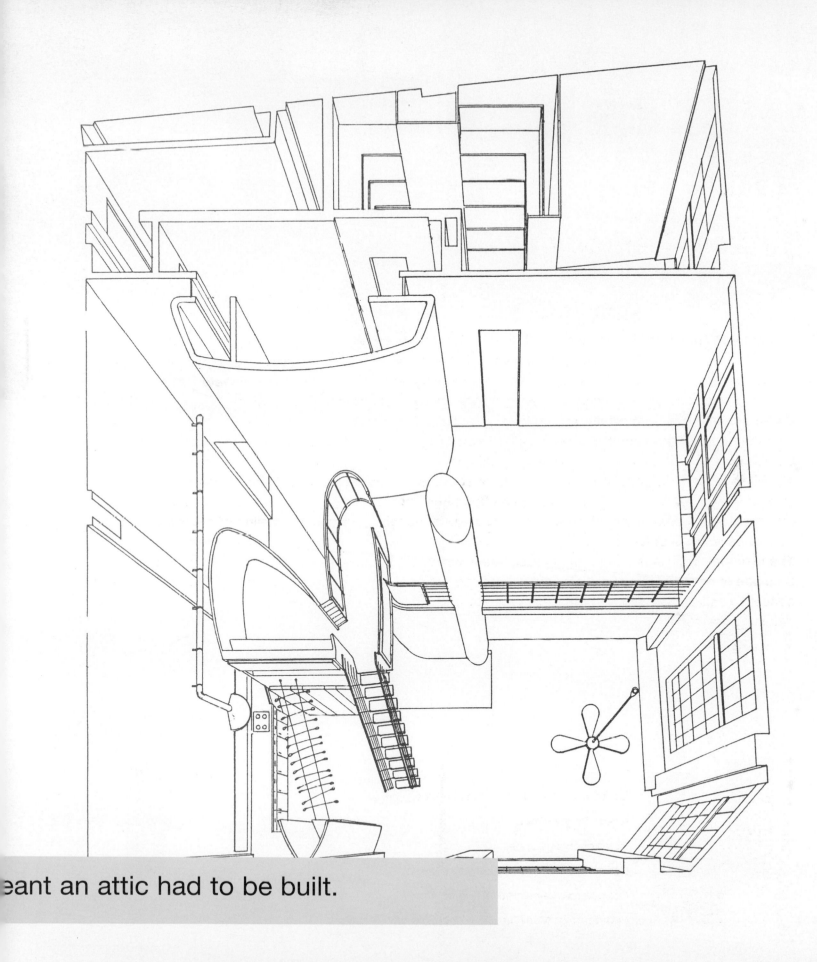

eant an attic had to be built.

The living room on the ground floor has been thought out to receive visitors.
The attic has been reserved as a family zone, where they can eat and watch TV

The steel stair alludes to OMA's dance theater in Amsterdam and has a steel spine structure.

The children's bedroom is on the ground floor with an almost direct access to the entrance. The couple's bedroom is in the attic, the point of the dwelling furthest away from the entrance.

Lower level.

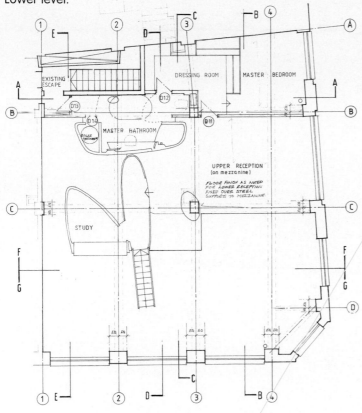

EXISTING ESCAPE

DRESSING ROOM   MASTER BEDROOM

MASTER BATHROOM

UPPER RECEPTION
(on mezzanine)

FLOOR FINISH AS NOTED
FOR LOWER RECEPTION
FIXED OVER STEEL
SUPPORTS TO MEZZANINE

STUDY

The kitchen runs along one side of the space with a 'utility pod' partly separating it from the rest of the room. This free-standing sculptural element conceals storage and a washing machine on the lower level and forms a circular study space above the point where it adjoins the mezzanine.

Uper level.

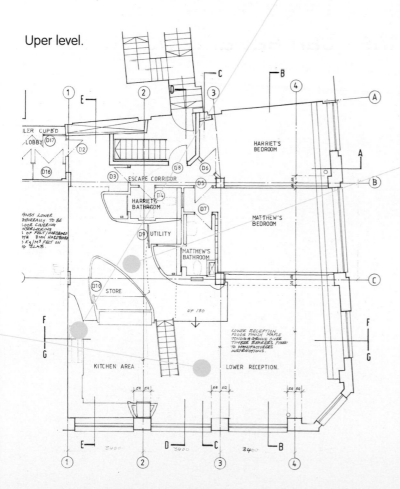

ILER CUPB'D
LOBBY

HARRIET'S BEDROOM

ESCAPE CORRIDOR

HARRIET'S BATHROOM

UTILITY

MATTHEW'S BEDROOM

MATTHEW'S BATHROOM

FINISH LOWER
GENERALLY TO BE
FLOOR COVERING
INTERLOCKING
S OF FELT/HARDBOARD
TE 8 MM HARDBOARD
KG/M3 FELT ON
SLAB

STORE

UP 130

LOWER RECEPTION.
FLOOR FINISH MAPLE
TONGUE GROOVE OVER
TIMBER BEARERS FIXED
TO MANUFACTURERS
INSTRUCTIONS.

KITCHEN AREA   LOWER RECEPTION.

Vertical Loft

An Attic in Barcelona

Pere Cortacans

▶ The building is located in Barcelona's Born district, an area of narrow, irregular, damp streets, and consists of a turn-of-the-century, L-shaped block surrounding an old sign-making workshop.
The modernization, carried out under the orders of Pere Cortacans, involved totally renovating the building and turning the old workshop into a central garden. Cortacans himself reserved one of the flats on the top floor for his own use.
His flat has three levels: the original level, an attic which resulted from the dismantling of the lower part of a ventilation space, and a glassed-in studio occupying the roof and giving access to the adjoining terrace.
This living space is configured vertically, with each level conceived for different activities so that the feelings of privacy and intensity contrast with each other.

LOCATION: Cortines 6, Barcelona, Spain.

CLIENT: Pere Cortacans.

AREA: 5,500 sq. ft. (510 sq. m).

COMPLETION DATE: 1998.

PHOTOGRAPHY: David Cardelús.

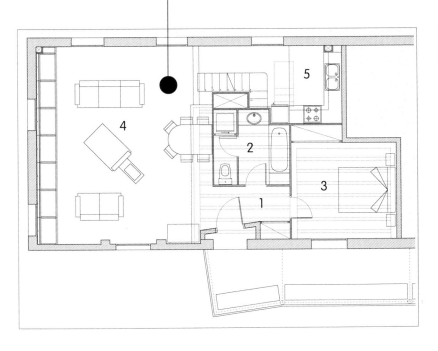

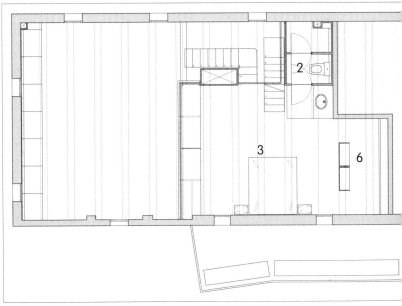

Lower floor.

Mezzanine.

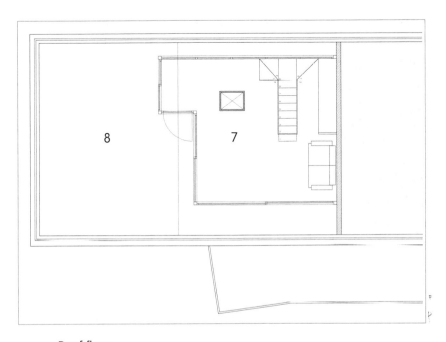

1. Entrance
2. Bathroom
3. Bedroom
4. Lounge
5. Kitchen
6. Dressing room
7. Study
8. Study

Roof floor.

Two structural elements of the building stand out: the impressive ceiling of roof beams made from melis pine brought from Cuba at the turn of the century, and the metal profiles painted with metallic oxide, which support the attic and the casing of the stairs.

Close to the ceiling, the stairs must adapt to the spaces of the beam fill.

Each of the three levels house different types of activities.

The bedroom and lounge are separated by a combined shelf/
seating unit with a small rail.

The studio has impressive views overlooking surrounding roofs that are typical of the
city's old district. Although the area's streets are dark and narrow, the flat is
nevertheless bathed in Mediterranean sunlight.

White and Void

Underwood Street Loft

Hugh Broughton Architects

▶ Four interconnected, former industrial buildings, facing onto Shepherdess Walk and Underwood Street, had been converted to provide warehouse-style apartments. Each loft was fitted out with the bare essentials of water, electricity, gas, kitchen sink, toilet, and hand basin. A lobby was built at the entrance of each loft to satisfy building regulations.

In the 1,600-square-foot loft of the second floor of Building 4, Hugh Broughton Architects have created a restrained and crisply detailed apartment with open-plan living space, kitchen, and dining area. Bedrooms and bathrooms have been enclosed to create privacy. A linear spine with a lower suspended ceiling hides the electrical and ventilation services from view.

The spine divides the living room and bedrooms from the more utilitarian spaces—the kitchen, hall, cloakroom, and bathroom. The bathroom protrudes from the spine with a knife-shaped wall, accentuating the sculptural impact on the open-plan areas. This wall thickens out to create a concealed cupboard space. When the door to the cupboard is opened, it screens the second guest bedroom from the living area. The ceiling to the protrusion is lower than the open-plan areas and is finished in white laminated glass, allowing a diffuse light to illuminate the plastered ceiling above.

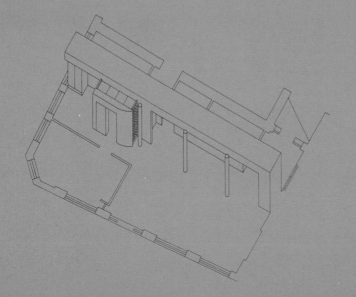

LOCATION: Underwood Street, London.

CLIENTS: Dominic and Emma Good.

COST: £ 35,000.

AREA: 1,590 sq. ft. (148 sq. m).

COMPLETION DATE: 1997.

DESIGN TEAM: Hugh Broughton Architects.

GENERAL CONTRACTOR: Summit Views.

PHOTOGRAPHY: Carlos Domínguez.

It is in the living room, the kitchen, and in the dining room where it is easiest to notice the industrial past of the building, both because of its diaphanous aspect and because of the brick walls and the cast iron pillars. Doors have not been put into this zone. There is continuity between the kitchen and the dining room. The lounge has been separated visually from the kitchen with a wall which does not break the spatial fluidity.

A restrained palette of new materials—white walls and ceilings, and an acid-etched glass-block wall—compliment the richness of the original brickwork and the Opepe African hardwood floors to create a dynamic and welcoming living environment.

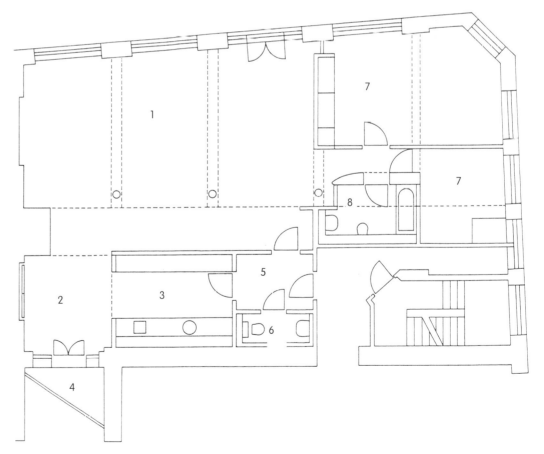

General floor plan.

1. Living area
2. Dining area
3. Kitchen
4. Balcony
5. Hall
6. Toilet
7. Bedroom
8. Bathroom

Low Cost = High Freedom

Derbyshire Street Residence

Fraser Brown MacKenna Architects

▶ Fraser Brown MacKenna was asked to refurbish the top two floors of a converted industrial loft in Bethnal Green. A dramatic, barrel-vaulted Perspex roof had been added to the building but spaces within were subdivided and dark.

A translucent floor was provided within a double-height space to allow the top floor to be used as the main living/kitchen and eating level. The lower floor was stripped out and opened up to provide a large and flexible level for sleeping, working, living, and utility.

On the lower floor a ten-meter-long, full-height Plexiglas screen divides storage and utility space from the main circulation and living areas in the building. In contrast to the bare expanse of the existing wood floor whose iron grilles and grooves recall the previous life of the loft space, the white screen which divides and shapes the space is strikingly clean and bright. This screen is both reflective and light absorbent. Beside the screen a hundred hues play on the simple geometry of the copper-clad storage area. A sculptural balustrade to the open stairs extends the copper treatment to the approach from the entrance below.

LOCATION: Derbyshire Street, London.

CLIENTS: Pascal Volle and Marta Wohrle.

AREA: 1,730 sq. ft. (160 sq. m).

TERRACE: 430 sq. ft. (40 sq. m).

COST: £ 22,806.

COMPLETION DATE: 1998.

DESIGN TEAM: Simon Fraser, Angus Brown, Martin MacKenna (principals), Diana Hare, Melanie Clear (assistants).

GENERAL CONTRACTOR: Envirozone, Ltd.

PHOTOGRAPHY: Nick Hufton/VIEW.

The screen can be manipulated quietly to modify space and to accommodate the lifestyles of the residents. The screen employs a bold language expressed in the stainless steel socket cap-head screws and aluminum T-sections.

1. Studio
2. Store
3. Bathroom
4. Balustrade
5. Stairs
6. Bedroom
7. Kitchen
8. Dining room
9. Living room
10. Terrace

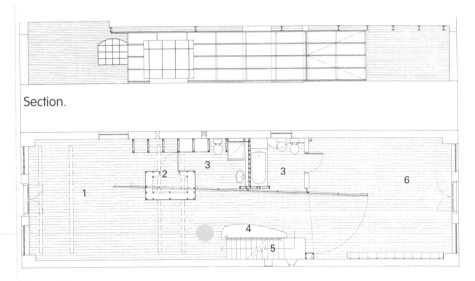

Section.

Upper floor.

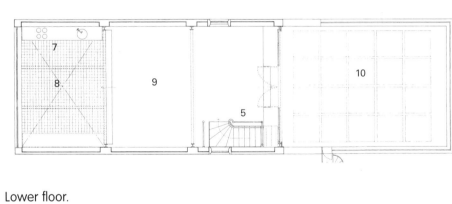

Lower floor.

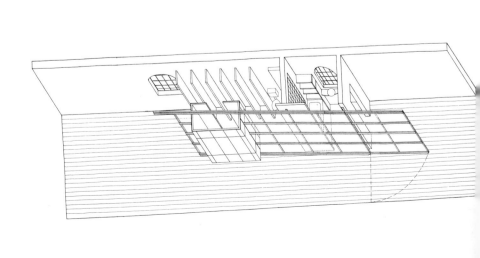

The simple shapes created by the screen, box, sink, and walls, which are formed from glass blocks or perforated metal, acknowledge the loft space and its prior life. These shapes encourage a way of life that celebrates the space and fosters a joyful presence within it.

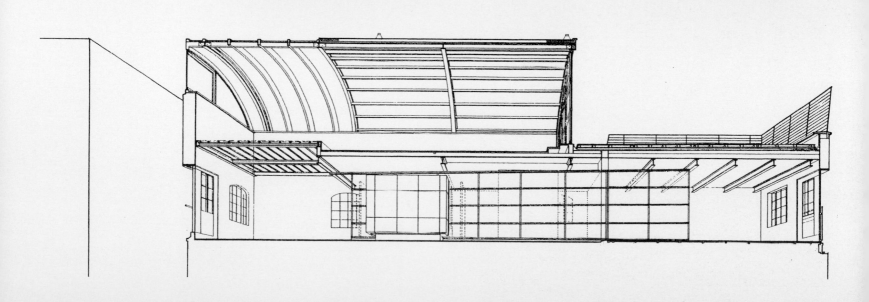

Designer Style

Loft in Bruges

Non Kitch Group

▶ Without a doubt, the most decisive factor in the successful conversion of this old can-making factory in Bruges, Belgium, into a living space was the remodeling of the roof, formed by a lattice structure with a saw-tooth profile which supports traditional tiling. William Sweetlove and Linda Arschoot, the designers of the Non Kitch Group, decided to substitute each of the northern-facing parallel strips of the roof with glass. The result not only lets in much more natural light, but also gives it the feel of an exterior plaza, given the considerable height of the space—almost 20 feet. On the lower floor, the living room opens onto a small garden with a covered swimming pool on one side, once again emphasizing the exterior, which is visible throughout the dwelling.

The loft occupies three levels, with a large central room rising the whole height of the dwelling. A mezzanine floor surrounding this central room contains the kitchen, dining room, bar, and TV room. Three steps below the living room are the billiard room, the bedroom, dressing room, gym, and the bathroom, which connects directly with the covered swimming pool.

LOCATION: Bruges, Belgium.

AREA: 6,450 sq. ft.

DATE: 1998.

DESIGN TEAM: William Sweetlove, Linda Arschoot.

PHOTOGRAPHY: Jan Verlinde.

The old factory chimney can be seen through the parallel skylights of the roof.

The construction of the mezzanine allows for spaces to have different scales within the same dwelling. The large central living room has the feel of a domestic public space. The other rooms are grouped around this almost plaza-like central living space and have balconies that look onto it. In this way, the hierarchical relationships of the spaces are boldly established.

In contrast to the asceticism of minimalist designers, the Non Kitch Group consider themselves as inheritors of the humor and colorful aesthetic of the Memphis group.

Many of the accessories and decorative elements of the loft have an unabashedly industrial look—for example, the stairway of galvanized steel, the central heating pipes, the lights, and the free-standing oven.

The furniture is carefully selected and includes items by Ettore Sottsass, Philippe Starck, Boris Sipek, Jean Nouvel, Norman Foster, and the architects themselves.

One of the factors influencing the design was the wish to create the ideal space to display the art collection of the owners, which includes works by Enrico de Paris, Mario de Brabandene, Niki de St. Phalle, Lindstrom, and Sweetlove. The light entering through the skylights is, not coincidentally, a feature of many art galleries and museums.

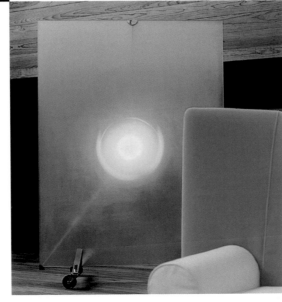

1. Garden
2. Covered pool
3. Living room
4. Office
5. Billiard room
6. Master bedroom
7. Dressing room
8. Bathroom
9. Bedroom
10. TV room
11. Bar
12. Ladder
13. Kitchen
14. Dining room

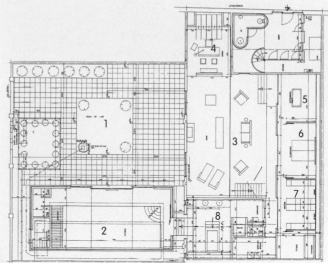

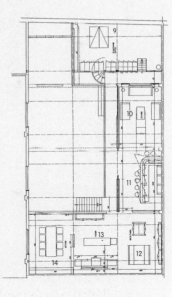

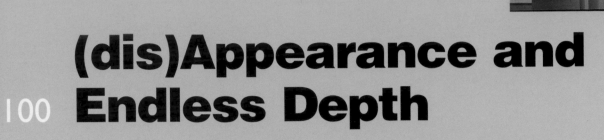

(dis)Appearance and Endless Depth

Holley Loft

Thomas Hanrahan + Victoria Meyers

▶ This project in lower Manhattan is an adaptation of an existing 3,800-square-foot industrial loft into a residence. The spatial characteristics of this project manifest an architecture constructed from the ideas of appearance and disappearance. It is composed of objects in full view and elements that recede deeply into space—to the point of seeming to disappear. This relationship between the objective view and the momentary view at the point of disappearance is a reflection of the active positioning and mobility of the body in a complex visual field. In material terms, appearance and disappearance are explored in the interaction between the solid wooden storage cabinets and the extensive use of glass. The design process was relatively long and interesting, as the client had a sophisticated knowledge of architecture and design. After many proposals and large-scale models, the final project assumed a decentralized and radically open character. In the final design there are no opaque walls. At any moment, from any position, the intention is for all elements to be distributed freely in the form of low cabinets and movable panels.

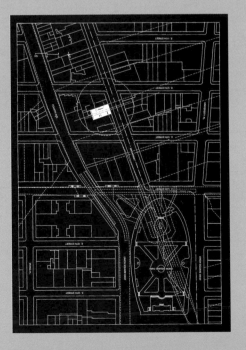

LOCATION: Manhattan, New York City.

CLIENT: Steve Holley.

AREA: 3,800 sq. ft. (350 sq. m).

COMPLETION DATE: 1996.

DESIGN TEAM: Thomas Hanrahan, Victoria Meyers (principals),
Martha Coleman, James Slade.

CONSULTANTS: M.A. Rubiano (mechanical engineer).

CONTRACTOR: Jauda Construction, Inc.

PHOTOGRAPHY: Peter Aaron/ESTO.

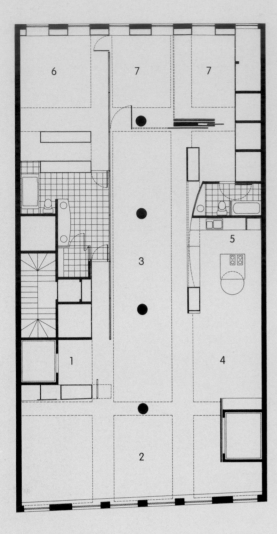

General plan.

1. Entrance
2. Living room
3. Gallery
4. Dinning room
5. Kitchen
6. Bedroom
7. Bedroom

The apartment is the single floor of a cast iron and terra cotta building built in 1875.

Light from both ends of the apartment penetrates deep into the residence, and movable panels allow for the creation of smaller, more intimate spaces for accommodating overnight guests.

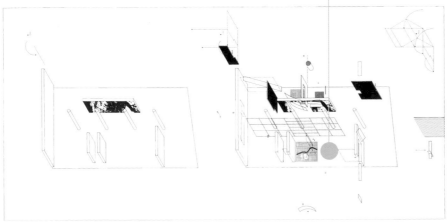

A single, full-height wall of glass and steel marks the major division of master bedroom and bathroom from the rest of the apartment.

The wooden cabinets and floor are maple, with limestone and marble counters. The movable panels are painted wood, while the glass-and-steel partitions are constructed from cold-rolled stock fabricated on site.

Industrial Structure

House in Igualada

Pep Zazurca

▶ This house in Igualada has a simple, rectangular form like a box. Steel columns and a steel truss support the roof, which spans over its entire width of 10 metres. This structure was prepared off site in a workshop and then installed by crane, which saved a geat del of time. The walls ahave been filled in with brick as a contrast to the steel, which illustrates the dislogue that Zazurca proposes between old and new building methods of building. Likewise a kind of dichotomy exists between the domestic role of this house and its obviously industrial references.

Zazurca's treatment of the side and rear walls places the design firmly back in the industrial mould: in a brilliant example of his daring he opted for Cor-ten cladding, giving the distinctive rusty look.

LOCATION: Igualada, Spain.

SIZE: 150 m².

DESIGNER: Pep Zazurca.

COMPLETION DDATE: 1997.

PHOTOGRAPHY: Eugeni Pons.

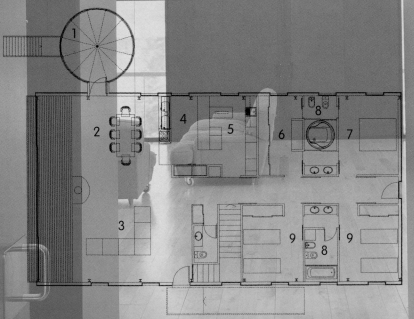

First floor.

1. Library
2. Dining room
3. Living room
4. Kitchen
5. Larder
6. Dressing room
7. Main bedroom
8. Bathroom
9. Bedroom

All over the house there is a parquet flooring, except in the kitchen where treated concrete adds some character. In the bedrooms a false thin wood ceiling has been installed. It offers thermal and acoustic isolation.

All the installations have been left visible.

The divisions between the bedrooms have been made with DIM panels.

Remodeling a Silversmith's Workshop

Lee House

Derek Wylie

▶ Lee House is in Clerkenwell, on the western fringe of the City of London, one of the world's financial capitals. The site, virtually derelict at the time the architect found it, had comprised a four-story shop and apartment facing St. John Street, and a two-story silversmith's workshop at the rear. These were separated by a small yard. The whole site occupied 450 square meters. Encircled by neighboring buildings, the deep and narrow site at the rear had limited views out and little natural light.

The clients were a young couple with two boys aged 8 and 10. The father owned a construction company and had himself been involved in building various well-known houses and interiors. The basic brief was to create a contemporary home suited to both work and family life which would reflect the urban grain of the site. The clients decided to split the site into two units, one of which could be sold to contribute to the overall development cost.

A natural split between the two residences was achieved by separating off the upper two levels of the St. John Street building. The clients' family house occupies the entire ground floor of the site, along with the rear first floor workshop area and basement of the St. John Street building, providing a total of 250 square meters of floor space.

LOCATION: St. John Street, Clerkenwell, London.

CLIENT: Martin Lee.

AREA: 4,850 sq. ft (450 sq. m).

COMPLETION DATE: 1997.

DESIGN TEAM: Derek Wylie (principal), Carl Harper,
Mike Neal (assistants).

GENERAL CONTRACTOR: Martin Lee.

PHOTOGRAPHY: Nick Kane, except kitchen by Mainstream and
courtyard balcony detail by Derek Wylie.

Clerkenwell was a thriving artisan quarter for over a hundred years. Following a rapid decline during the 1950s, the area is now experiencing a renaissance, attracting new urban development and a young, trend-conscious population.

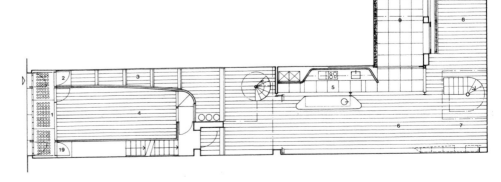

Basement.

Ground floor plan.

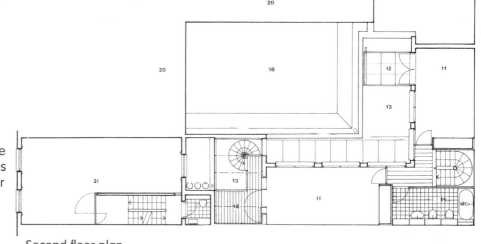

The design approach was to expose the shell of each of the original buildings and create a new home with spaces flowing informally into each other while maximizing opportunities for natural light.

1. Street lobby
2. House entrance
3. Stepped ramp
4. Office
5. Kitchen
6. Dining
7. TV Den
8. Living
9. Courtyard
10. Pool
11. Bedroom
12. Balcony
13. Void
14. Bathroom
15. Mezzanine
16. Sauna room
17. Utility
18. Adjoining roof
19. Apartment entrance
20. Adjoining properties
21. Apartment first floor

Second floor plan.

Detailed discussions of "how we live" revealed a belief in spatial democracy, and so it was clear that this concept should inform the organization of the house. Of particular concern was how the house could be used equitably and sensibly by both children and adults.

ST. JOHN ST.

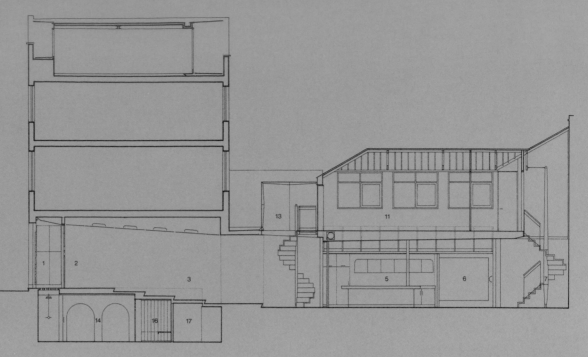

At first floor level the bathroom includes a storage wall constructed from aluminum channel sections and a painted wooden ladder frame with overlapping doors to throw off water. The wall provides 25 compartments for clothes, linen, and vanity stations.

The new construction is deliberately robust to withstand the wear and tear of family life, while the detailing is precise to contrast with the roughness of the existing shell. A new, boarded oak floor has been laid throughout the ground level, including the stepped entrance ramp, to emphasize the continuous spatial flow at this level from the front entrance to the rear courtyard. Similarly, limestone flooring spreads from the courtyard into the kitchen and dining areas.

Each of the new staircases has been placed to suggest physical separation between different living areas without corrupting the continuity of the space.

Working in a Loft

A Loft with Garden

Casadesús House

Antoni Casadesús

▶ Antoni Casadesús has remodeled the premises formerly occupied by a textile firm and has converted it into a space capable of holding both his studio of interior design as well as his private living space. Several factors make this an excellent location, including the dimensions of the premises (about 1,500 sq. ft. combined with its great height), a rear patio oriented to the southeast, and above all its proximity of only a few meters from Passeig de Gràcia in the center of Barcelona. A central strip with a small garden and the kitchen separates the most private area of the loft—the bedroom, bathroom, and attic—from a large space on two floors which opens onto the rear patio-garden. This layout allows separation of the different functions and of the different degrees of privacy, while at the same time maintaining a visual connection between all points of the loft. From the entrance, both the intermediate garden and the rear terrace can be seen.

In spite of the considerable depth of the premises, natural light is present everywhere. Almost all the surfaces, including the floor and some pieces of furniture—a sofa, shelves, piano, and table—are either white or in pale shades.

LOCATION: Consell de Cent 320, Barcelona.

CLIENT: Antoni Casadesús.

AREA: 1,500 sq. ft. (140 sq. m).

COMPLETION DATE: 1998.

PHOTOGRAPHY: Eugeni Pons.

124

The sofa, the center table, and the shelving are designed by

adesús himself.

General floor plan.

1. Entrance
2. Bathroom
3. Bedroom
4. Garden
5. Kitchen
6. Living room/studio
7. Patio
8. Mezzanine

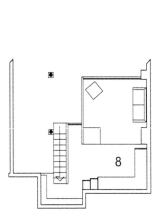

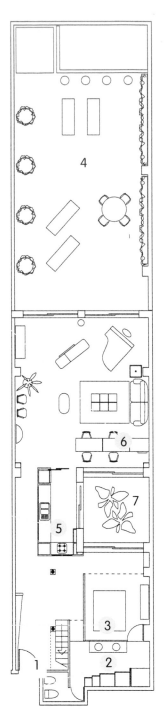

The flooring is of white marble throughout, except in the attic, which is floored with teak.
The work chairs are a Charles Eames design, while the table is by Isern and Bernal.

Polished, bright surfaces dominate the bathroom. The taps are designed by Philippe Starck.

The original structure of pillars and beams of wrought iron has been painted a dark color which contrasts with the other finishes used.

The Aluminum Wall

Miller-Jones Studio

LOT/EK

▶ Located in the garment district in Midtown Manhattan, the Miller-Jones Studio is a result of the conversion of a commercial loft into the residence/work space for a fashion photographer and a set designer. The loft, on the 14th floor, enjoys southern exposure and exciting Manhattan cityscapes through a 30-foot-long window. After returning the space to its industrial frame of reference (high ceiling, concrete floor, and white walls), a bidimensional element (the side of a 40-foot-long aluminum shipping container) is inserted to define a shear edge between private and professional needs. The container wall cuts across the warehouse space and intersects different functions along its axis. Only technological appliances emerge when it is completely closed. A system of incisions breaks it into a mechanism of rotating panels that, when opened, reestablish the continuity of the spaces revealed behind them: bedroom, kitchen, and storage.

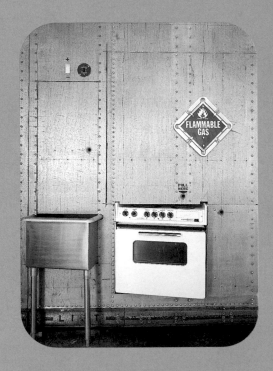

LOCATION: 35th Street, Manhattan, New York City.

CLIENTS: Steven Miller and Christine Jones.

AREA: 2,000 sq. ft. (186 sq. m).

COMPLETION DATE: 1996.

DESIGN TEAM: Ada Tolla, Giuseppe Lignano.

PHOTOGRAPHY: Paul Warchol.

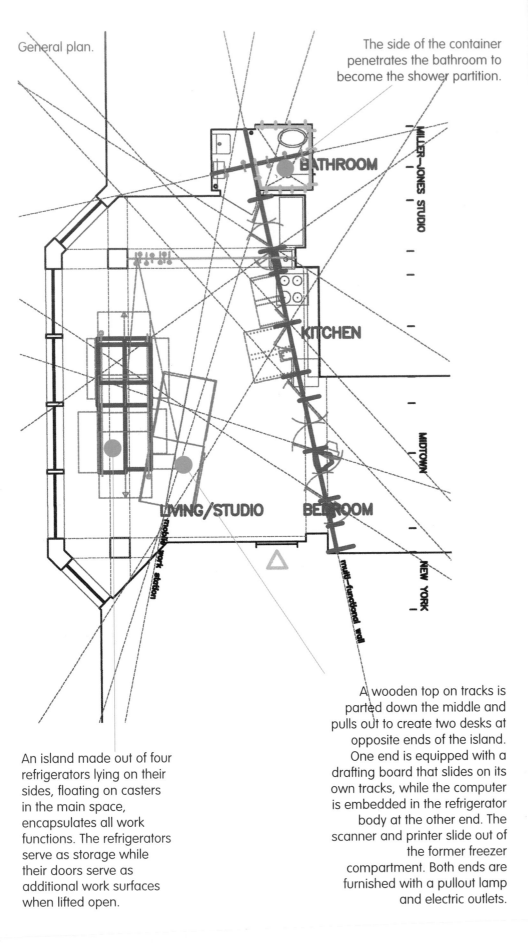

General plan.

The side of the container penetrates the bathroom to become the shower partition.

BATHROOM

MILLER–JONES STUDIO

KITCHEN

MIDTOWN

LIVING/STUDIO

BEDROOM

mobile work station

multi-functional wall

NEW YORK

An island made out of four refrigerators lying on their sides, floating on casters in the main space, encapsulates all work functions. The refrigerators serve as storage while their doors serve as additional work surfaces when lifted open.

A wooden top on tracks is parted down the middle and pulls out to create two desks at opposite ends of the island. One end is equipped with a drafting board that slides on its own tracks, while the computer is embedded in the refrigerator body at the other end. The scanner and printer slide out of the former freezer compartment. Both ends are furnished with a pullout lamp and electric outlets.

A Russian Doll

An Architect's Studio in Madrid

Enrique Bardají

▶ Enrique Bardají designed his own studio in a building that had also been designed by this Madrid architect. He participated in every phase of its design and construction while playing the role of both client and designer.

Both the building and studio have an intentionally industrial character, with simple finishes and with their structure and installations exposed. The spatial layout of the studio is essentially a central space with a large area and height, and has a layout designed to facilitate teamwork.

Another important element in the design is light. A central skylight, covered by a canvas which diffuses the direct light, illuminates the large, central area. In addition, three of the perimeter walls contain full-length windows protected by Venetian blinds that follow the sun's path throughout the day.

LOCATION: Manuel Tovar 25, Madrid, Spain.

CLIENT: Enrique Bardají.

CONSTRUCTION DATE: 1997.

DESIGN TEAM: Enrique Bardají (architect), José Manuel Miralles (design), Hendrik Hiddermann (work director), Juan José Ruiz (site architect).

CONSULTANTS: NB-35 (structures), J&G Ingenieros (installations).

PHOTOGRAPHY: Lionel Malka.

Escala: 1/100

Escala: 1/100

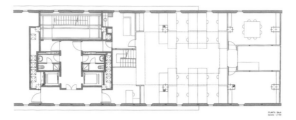

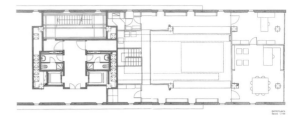

Ground floor.
A library, meeting room, machine room, and kitchen/dining room are built around the central space.

Upper floor.
The filing space and Enrique Bardají's own office are located in this raised area.

The central space houses general design activities. The floor is blue linoleum, 3.5 mm thick, the walls and ceilings are painted white, while the exposed structure is finished in a light gray.

For Bardají, empty space is one of the most important design elements in architecture.

Section.

The work tables, designed by the German architect Egor Eiermann, are large enough to allow designers to work with computer and paper at the same time. The furniture along the sides of the space were specially designed for the studio by Bardají himself.

The technical drawing rooms in the southern area and the offices to the north are divided by a glass wall with thick wooden frames. The transparency of this wall, together with the light streaming in from the skylight in the ceiling and numerous other openings in the walls, ensures that natural light reaches all corners of the building.

The air conditioning ducts, made of galvanized sheet steel, have also been left exposed.

The upper area has a base formed by two sheets that contain isolating material and are finished with linoleum. They are supported by a structure of metal beams.

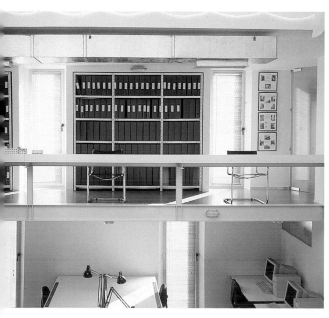

New Design for Old Factories

German Design Center

Sir Norman Foster & Partners

▶ Essen, situated in the heart of Germany's largest urban area, is a city characterized by mining and manufacturing. These heavy industries are declining and new uses are needed for the legacy of industrial buildings. That was the challenge presented at Zeche Zollverein, where one magnificent building in a decommissioned coal mining complex has been adapted by Foster and Partners to create a new home for the German Design Center, which has been established to promote contemporary design in Germany and abroad.

The brief called for the preservation of the listed boiler house and the creation of the new center within its shell, creating exhibition spaces, offices, and conference facilities. The German Design Center displays both temporary and permanent exhibitions which are constantly being updated, therefore requiring highly flexible galleries. The challenge was to contrast the powerful aesthetic of the industrial architecture with contemporary architecture and also to create a sympathetic backdrop for the Design Center's exhibitions.

LOCATION: Essen, Germany.

CLIENT: Bauhütte Zeche Zollverein Schacht XII Gmbh.

COMPLETION DATE: 1997.

DESIGN TEAM: Norman Foster, David Nelson, Paul Kalkhoven, Stefan Behling, Reinhard Joecks.

CONSULTANTS: Ove Arup (structural engineers/new construction), Weber, Hamelmann, Surmann (structural engineers/old construction), Ingenieurbüro G Hoffmann (mechanical), Stredich and partners (electrical), Búro Böll und Krabel (cladding and site supervision).

PHOTOGRAPHY: Nigel Young.

Cross-section.

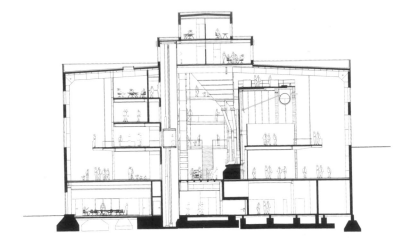

Level 1.   Level 4.

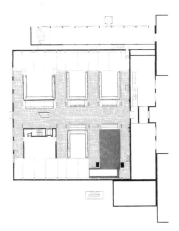   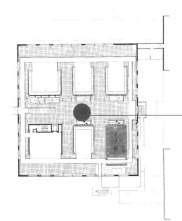

Longitudinal section.

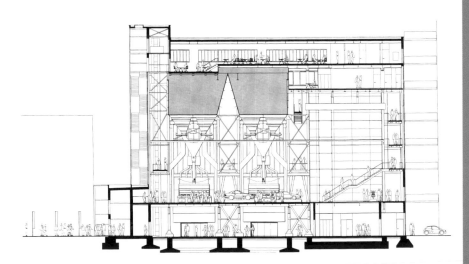

The complex was originally designed by the architects Fritz Schupp and Martin Kremmer between 1927 and 1932, but was closed down in 1986 when coal production became economically unviable.

These industrial buildings all share a common vocabulary of reddish brown, exposed steel-beams with industrial glazing and red brick. During construction, the building's facade was rebuilt and a number of later additions were removed to reveal its original elegance and splendor. The chimney, which had become unstable, was demolished before the start of the project.

The centerpiece is the boiler house, an imposing structure with an interior hall of cathedral-like grandeur.

Inside, the heavy industrial feel of the building has been conserved by leaving much of the historical structure exposed and unrestored.

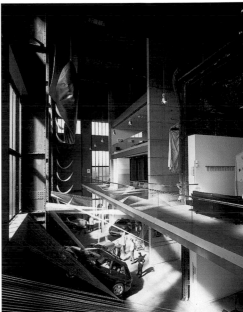

Visitors enter into the dramatic central hall where the rusty steel structure and exposed brick walls rise up on each side to show the building's industrial heritage. One boiler is preserved intact as an example of 1930s technology for future generations. The other four large boilers have been gutted and two floors of galleries added, providing a blank canvas for exhibitions while still revealing the upper portions of the boilers. These galleries are accessible from the outer edges and are linked to each other by a walkway with glass balustrades.

Grids and Patterns

Architects Working for Engineers in Chicago

Valerio Dewalt Train Architects

▶ What type of office space is appropriate for engineers, the keepers of rational thought in a world full of ambiguity? One answer to this question began with an individual workstation designed to maximize efficiency and support the latest technological resources. The workstations were designed around the tools used by the engineering staff. Each station had to accommodate computers, drawings, and reference materials. The workstation walls are low to facilitate project team and interdepartmental communication. The station itself became a module that was mirrored again and again to form a grid of blocks and streets.

The design provides fifty-five custom-designed workstations in an open room punctuated by enclosed service towers housing copiers, printers, and libraries. Center bays open to an eight-story atrium, at which point the service towers are twenty-two feet high.

At the edges of this grid, the module evolves to form large semiprivate offices and larger private offices. Where the grid ends, residual space provides a linear reception zone leading from the street entrance. Everything in the plan seems orderly and essential.

LOCATION: Chicago, Illinois.

CLIENT: WMA Consulting Engineers, Ltd.

COMPLETION DATE:1997.

AREA: 23,000 sq. ft. (2,150 sq. m).

DESIGN TEAM: Joseph M. Valerio (principal in charge/design principal), Neil Sheehan (project architect), Kasia Gawlik, Erica Pagel, Jason Hall, Marius Ronnett, Andrew To (assistants).

CONSULTANTS: WMA Consulting Engineers, Ltd.(mechanical/electrical engineering).

GENERAL CONTRACTOR: The Kaiser Loftrium, Ltd.

PHOTOGRAPHY: Karant+Associates/Barbara Karant; Neil Sheehan (exterior building photo).

Axonometry.

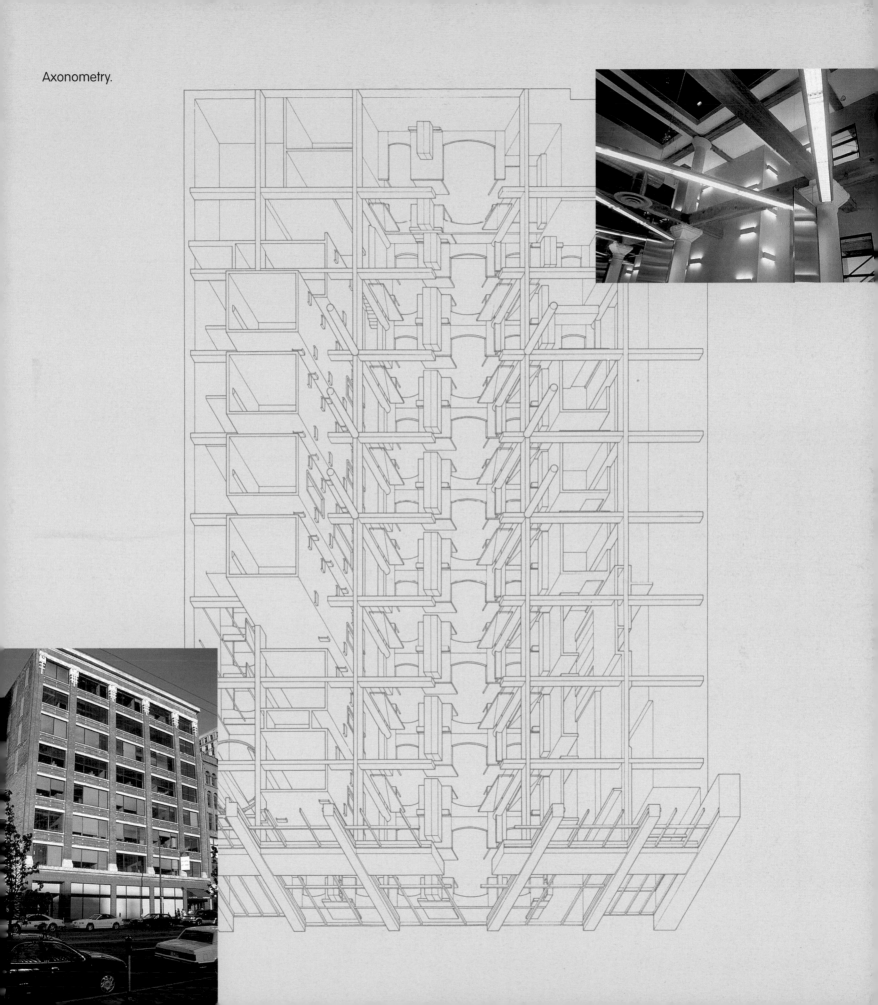

The need to fit as many workstations as possible into small structural bays with atypical dimensions, as well as the need to work within a modest project budget, was behind the decision to install custom-designed millwork furniture. To help keep costs low, this furniture was assembled with self-finished materials. Support panels and shelf units are constructed of exposed-edge Baltic birch plywood, which was dyed and finished with laquer. Work surface tops are raw MDF fiberboard finished with polyurethane.

The space is brought to life creatively and inexpensively by patterns of light. These are defined by indirect fixtures suspended in a diagonal layout, a medley of custom-fabricated light boxes arranged over all the walls, and suspended stainless steel panel workstation dividers. Exposed mechanical systems add to the rhythm and energy of the room.

Planta general.

1. Entrance
2. Reception
3. Library
4. Computer room
5. Kitchen
6. Offices
7. Meeting room
8. Reserved area
9. Stairs
10. Work room
11. Entries and exits
12. Warehouse
13. Machinery

Seen in three dimensions, everything in the office space seems exceptional. Lighting, HVAC, and sprinklers are planned on contrasting diagonal grids. Private office enclosures, bland when seen in the two-dimensional plan, become building-like icons extending vertically through the second floor, dotted with a diamond grid of implicit windows.

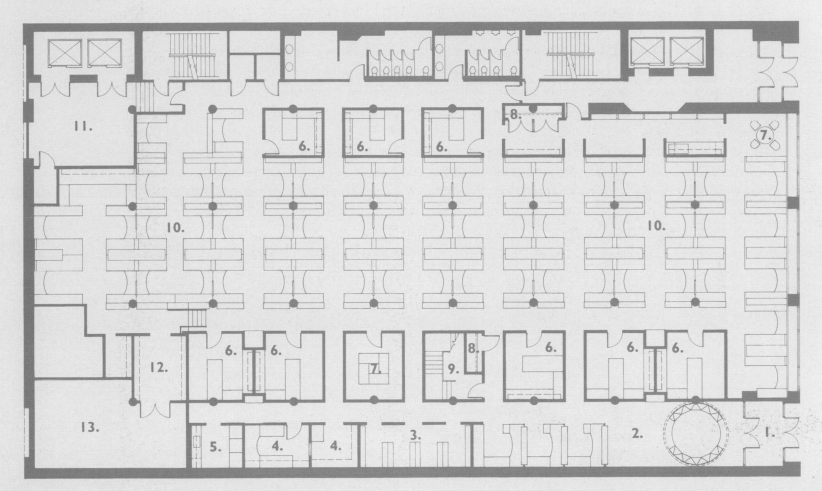

The offices are located on the first two floors of an eight-story building.

A Tempting Roughness

Remodeling a Warehouse in Amsterdam

de architectengroep

▶ For the architectengroep the upper five stories of the premises were ideal, once they had been radically renovated. As a result of renovations the original character of the building had largely disappeared. The westerdokhuis was originally a warehouse that supplied the bakeries of Amsterdam with flour.

The point of departure for the design was the division of the building into a northern and southern zone, with the central corridor forming part of the drawing room. The wall between these two zones is made of timber frames, with several different types of glass panels. Subsequently, sunlight can enter even the northern rooms. The skylight in the roof and the voids intensify this effect.

The roughness and solidity of the materials and details is a response to the original character of this flour warehouse—a robust, factory-like building. This choice of materials also represents a resistance to the established standards and meticulous-appearing construction methods seen throughout the Netherlands. The architectural firm's headquarters is the perfect location to display its work in practice.

LOCATION: Westerdokhuis, Amsterdam, Netherlands.

CLIENT: de architectengroep bv rijnboutt ruijssenaars hendriks van gameren mastenbroek.

COMPLETION DATE: 1998.

ARCHITECT: Bjarne Mastenbroek.

DESIGN TEAM: Willmar Groenendijk, Arnoud Gelauff, Floor Arons, Brian Boots. Michiel Raaphorst, Jan Oudeman, Sonja Uzelac, Cornelia Deszy, Mattias Ziems.

GENERAL CONTRACTOR: Bouwbedrijf M.J. de Nijs & Zn bv.

PHOTOGRAPHY: Christian Richters.

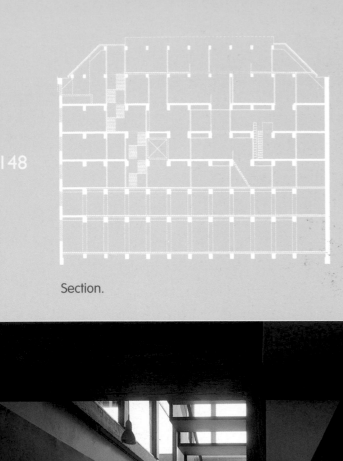

Section.

The separation between the south zone (the drawing rooms) and the north (offices) has been made with a glass wall supported by solid wood. The transparency achieved, added to the effect of the skylight, and the numerous light-filtering openings, enables daylight to reach all corners of the building.

The imperfections in the rough work were disguised with cheap building materials.

Attic.

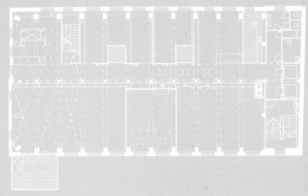

Third floor.

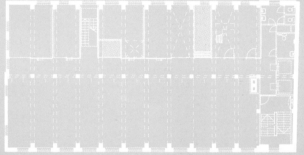

Remodeling an Old Bakery

Workshop in Glasgow

Anderson Christie Architects

▶ The existing property was an old bakery which had been derelict for about eight years, and is partly within a tenement block in the west end of Glasgow. The dilapidated building had considerable character—incorporating old cast iron bakers ovens, white glazed brick walls, and a steel frame structure. Architects saw a number of opportunities to intervene in the existing structure and to play with the volumes and spaces. The only problems were a limited budget and the need to spend much of the available money to make the building wind- and watertight.
The finishes have been deliberately left with a hard appearance. In certain areas Anderson and Christie have retained the rubble stone walls and glazed brickwork. They have lined the walls with insulated plasterboard only where necessary to keep the heat in and humidity out. New floors were needed because of the building's condition, and all are of varnished concrete. In contrast with the natural finishes, Anderson and Christie have given the new walls strong colors to create focus and life within the spaces.

LOCATION: 382 Great Western Road, Glasgow, United Kingdom.

CLIENT: Anderson Christie Architects.

COMPLETION DATE: 1997.

DESIGN TEAM: Anderson Christie Architects.

CONSULTANTS: A.M. Sidey & Associates (structural),
             Reid Associates (quantity surveyor.

GENERAL CONTRACTOR: Helforn Ltd.

METALWORK: Andrew Scott, Ewan Hunter, Simon Hopkins.

CARPENTER: John Wood.

INSTALLED PAINTINGS: Rowan Mace.

PHOTOGRAPHY: Andrew Lee.

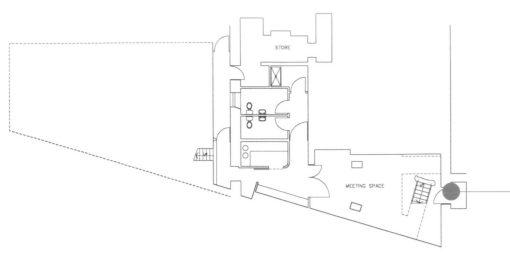

Ground floor.

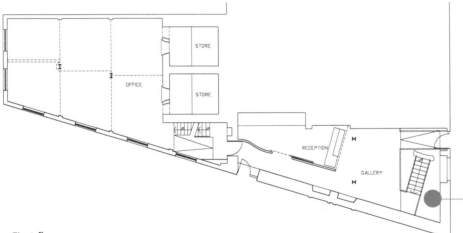

First floor.

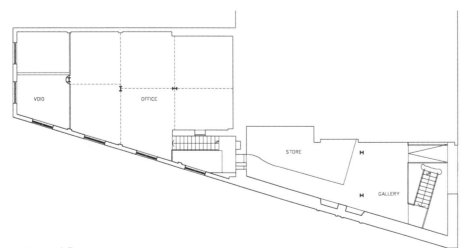

Second floor.

The studio space is linked to the street via a small shop within a Victorian tenement—previously the baker's shop. This fronts onto a main street into the city, Great Western Road, and accommodates the work space's reception area and client meeting room, which are the public areas. The drawing studio space, the working area, is accommodated within the actual bakery. The service accommodation, plant, lavatories, and printing room form a core at the heart of the plan, accessible by stairs from the drawing office.

The majority of accessories incorporated into the building were realised by metal workers or carpinters with whom Andersen and Christie had studied at the Glasgow School of Art.

Two double-height volumes have been created by removing sections of floor. These link related spaces together practically and visually. The main, north-facing drawing studio is linked to a meeting room below it. The reception area to the south is linked to the client meeting room, and the double-height gallery maximizes exposure to sunlight.

The meeting tables, shelving, and reception desk were designed by the architects and built by a local carpenter, John Wood.

A Generous Space

Williams Murray Banks

Pierre d'Avoine Architects

▶ Williams Murray Banks is a graphics and packaging design firm that has recently been set up by Richard Williams, Richard Murray, and Justin Banks. Their twenty-employee office is situated on the second floor of the Heal's Building in London's West End. The project involved fitting out two spaces: the main office (30 m long, 6.5 m wide, and 2.7 m high) and a smaller meeting room. WMB required the main office to be an adaptable space, generally open and democratic but capable of providing three cellular offices when the occasion demands, without losing the sense of openness.

Pierre d'Avoine Architects' design was evolved as a reading of the host space which emphasized its length and lowness as a virtue. The strategy included building a free-standing assemblage of elements placed along the central axis of the space, below a plywood bulkhead that has been lowered. The elements brought together under this ceiling constitute the majority of the accommodation: partitions, storage, desks, and sliding doors. Together they act as a linear measure to the host space.

The tight budget made it impossible to propose a design incorporating a usual mix of elements, materials, and finishes. In order to complete this 200-square-meter renovation within the financial constraints, all materials requiring finishes by skilled workers were ruled out, and birch-faced plywood was used throughout, such as for partitions, doors, furniture, and louvers.

LOCATION: Alfred Mews, London.

CLIENT: Williams, Murray, Banks.

COMPLETION DATE: 1997.

DESIGN TEAM: Pierre d'Avoine, Thomas Emerson.

CONTRACTOR: Finlon Building Contractors, Ltd.

PHOTOGRAPHY: David Grandgorge.

Open plan.

1. Entrance/reception
2. Conference room
3. Office
4. Designers area
5. Computer suite
6. Louvers

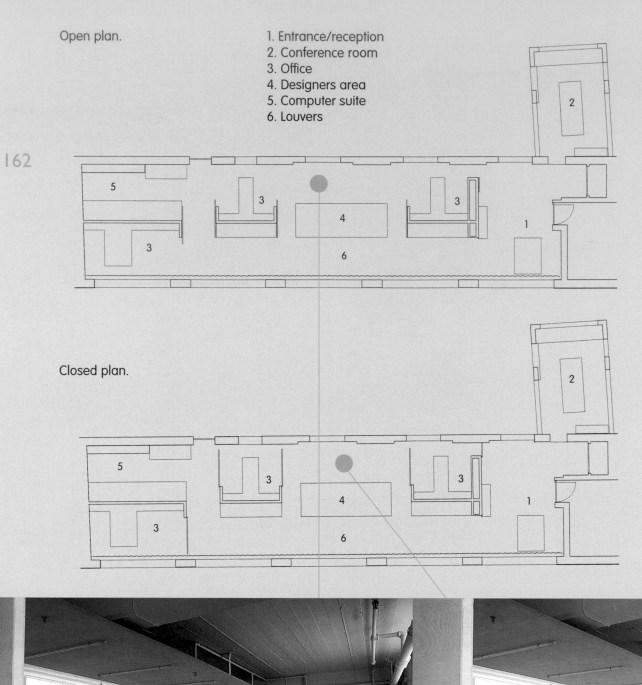

Closed plan.

Walls, furniture, doors, and louvers are made ambiguous. Walls and doors are similar in size, material, and construction. The sliding door, built without metal, has an architectural scale. The space is not transformed by opening and closing doors between separate rooms but rather by intervening directly with large sliding panels—which are neither door nor wall.

The long, south-facing wall is almost entirely glazed. In order to control sunlight and solar heat gain, plywood louvers line the wall along its entire length. The louvers are operated in groups of ten. The lowered bulkhead and the louvered screen define the public circulation and frame the primary view throughout the space.

The walls and ceiling of the interior shell have been repainted in a pale color, and the concrete floor has been sanded and finished with graphite lacquer.

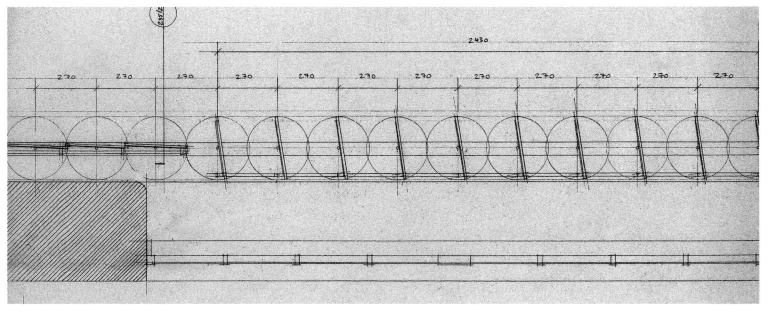

Images in Flux

Sunshine Interactive Network

Gates Merkulova Architects

▶ Sunshine Interactive Network (SIN) is a young, rapidly changing new-media company. Their search for new office space led to the 10,000-square-foot, full-floor loft building in Manhattan that had been converted to office use.

The company is comprised of five groups: film and video, music records, digital, distribution, and administration. Their activities range from media development through production and distribution, and require separate but not entirely distinct territories and common areas.

The architects' approach was to fill the volume with a dense arrangement of elements. The center of the space is occupied by three shapes containing shared functions: a thick-walled conic shape for small conferences and audiovisual demonstrations; a long, warped space for larger conferences and film/video viewing; and a room for film shoots and meetings. The shapes also serve to separate the territories of the various groups.

A recording studio and a video editing bay, both in use around the clock, are located to the side and are entered independently. The space is otherwise left open, with the perimeter windows admitting light to all the work areas. Partial-height, translucent fiberglass screens loosely partition the common space.

LOCATION: Broadway at Astor Place, New York City.

CLIENT: Sunshine Interactive Network.

AREA: 10,000 sq. ft. (930 sq. m).

COMPLETION DATE: 1998.

DESIGN TEAM: Paul Gates, Eugenia Merkulova.

CONSULTANTS: Athwal and Associates, Inc.
(mechanical engineer).

CONTRACTOR: Palais Enterprises, Inc.

ARCHITECTURAL WOODWORK: Woodweave, Inc.

PHOTOGRAPHY: J.B. Grant Photographs.

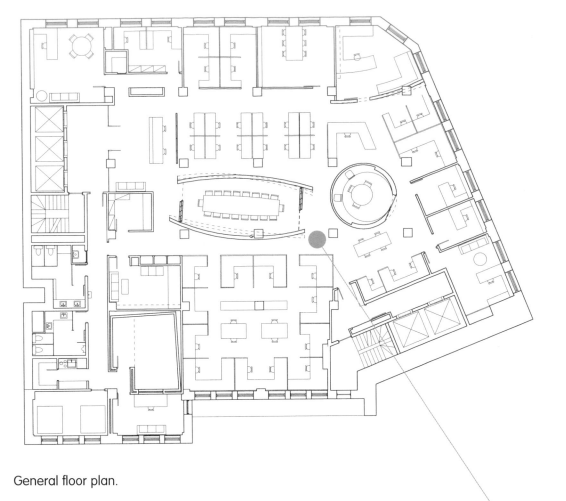

General floor plan.

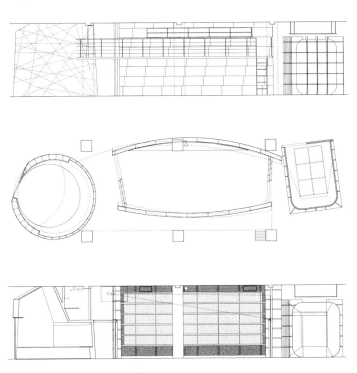

Detail of the three central rooms.

The nature of the company's project is such that the office population is in constant flux. The new space should be able to accommodate the regular employees needing workstations of their own, as well as various types of virtual and temporary workers. Spaces, therefore, have to be both territorial and nonterritorial, common and private, and flexible enough to adapt to the changes which are a condition of companies today. A fundamental idea behind the company itself was that a creative synergy would develop through the overlapping of boundaries between the various groups.

A grid of open trays that house communications wiring is suspended from the ceiling, providing easy access for rearrangement of computer cables.

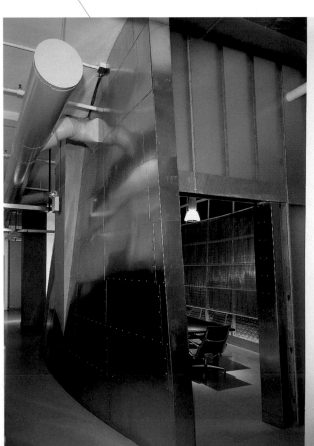

The Rhythm of Light

Studio in Tribeca

Parsons + Fernández-Casteleiro

▶ The design of the first converted space in an existing cast-iron-faced manufacturing building incorporated architectural gestures that served as guidelines for updating the remaining building spaces. Cast-concrete floors, vertical fluorescent light fixtures, and a palette of grays were developed as standards for rental and public spaces to be created through the five-story structure.
The new studio highlights the longitudinal axis of the existing floor plan and the plan's projection into outside street vistas.
A central bookcase spine containing all the power and telecommunications wiring links a common work area with private office/conference areas at either end. With their vertical placement and horizontal spacing, the fluorescent light fixtures continue the rhythm of the circulation as they reflect off one wall. Their placement creates subtle changes in illumination along the entire length of the space throughout the day. Incandescent and halogen fixtures on the central spine supplement the fluorescent lights, and are used to highlight exhibits and produce an entirely different atmosphere at night.

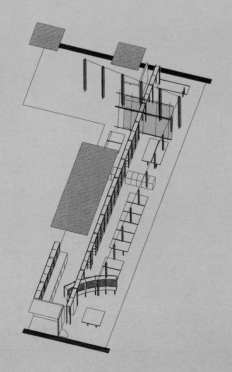

LOCATION: 62 White Street, New York City.

CLIENT: Parsons + Fernandez-Casteleiro.

AREA: 2,300 sq. ft. (214 sq. m).

COST: $30,000.

COMPLETION DATE: 1998.

DESIGN TEAM: Parsons + Fernandez-Casteleiro.

PHOTOGRAPHY: Paul Warchol.

Installing vertical flourescent
lighting spaced out evenly not only
allows the work tables and the
hanging plans and models to be
illuminated, it also gives the office
its own special rhythm. The effect
created by the flourescent lights
goes beyond its functionality: it is
a singular addition to the office
that reminds one of the
installations of James Turrell.

The floor is of polished concrete. The walls are white. The shelves and guiding rails are of mecano type metal. Parsons and Fernández-Casteleiro have used an industrial language in their design and materials that do not blow the budget.

General floor plan.

1. Reception
2. Spacious room
3. Office
4. Meeting room

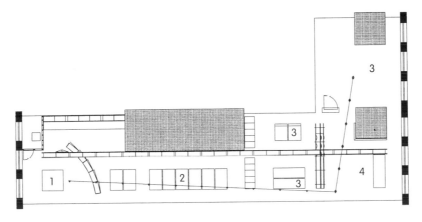

Directory

AEM Studio Ltd.

80 O'Donnell Court
Brunswick Centre. Brunswick Square
London WC1N 1NX.
United Kingdom
T. 0171 713 91 91
F. 0171 713 91 99

Anderson Christie Architects

382 Great Western Road
Glasgow G4 9HT. United Kingdom
T. 0141 339 15 15
F. 0141 339 05 05

Antoni Casadesús Estudi

Consell de Cent, 320
08007 Barcelona. Spain
T. 93 215 01 11
F. 93 215 01 11

Circus Architects

1 Summer's Street
London EC1R 5BD. United Kingdom
T. 0171 833 19 99
F. 0171 833 18 88

Cristian Cirici.
Carles Bassó Arquitectes

Pujades, 63
08005 Barcelona. Spain
T. 93 485 47 52
F. 93 309 67 48

CZWG Architects

17 Bowling Green Lane
London EC1R OBD. United Kingdom
T. 0171 253 25 23
F. 0171 253 05 94

de architectengroep

Barentsazplein 7
1013 NJ Amsterdam. Holland
T. 020 530 48 48
F. 020 530 48 00

Derek Wylie Architecture

112A Bon Marche Centre
444 brixton road. London SW9 8EJ
United Kingdom
T. 0171 274 63 73
F. 0171 274 14 49

Enrique Bardají,
Estudio de Arquitectura

Manuel Tovar, 25
28034 Madrid. Spain
T. 91 358 51 40
F. 91 358 52 05

Foster and Partners

Riverside Three
22 Hester Road
London SW11 4AN. United Kingdom
T. 0171 738 04 55
F. 0171 738 11 07/08

Fraser Brown MacKenna Architects

2 St. Johns Place
Clerkenwell
London EC1M 4DE. United Kingdom
T. 0171 251 05 43
F. 0171 251 05 17

Gates Merkulova Architects LLP

155 Avenue of the Americas, Suite 1202
New York, NY 10013. U.S.A
T. 212 675 07 90
F. 212 675 21 88

George Ranalli, Architect

150 West 28th Street
New York, NY 10001. U.S.A
T. 212 255 62 63
F. 212 255 10 49

Hugh Broughton Architects

4 Addison Bridge Place
London W14 8XP. United Kingdom
T. 0171 602 88 40
F. 0171 602 52 54

Joan Bach

Aribau, 239
08013 Barcelona. Spain
T. 93 246 68 01

LOT/EK

55 Little West 12 Street
New York, NY 10014. U.S.A
T. 212 255 93 26
F. 212 255 93 26

McDowell + Benedetti

62 Roserbery Avenue
London EC1R 4RR. United Kingdom
T. 0171 278 88 10
F. 0171 278 88 44

Non Kitch Group bvba

H. Deweertlaan 10/11
8670 Koksijde. Belgium
T. 58 52 09 85
F. 58 52 09 85

Orefelt Associates

4 Portobello Studios
5 Haydens Place
London W11 1LY. United Kingdom
T. 0171 243 31 81
F. 0171 792 11 26

Parsons + Fernandez-Casteleiro, PC

62 White Street
New York, NY 10013. U.S.A
T. 212 431 43 10
F. 212 431 44 96

Pep Zazurca

Ramon Miquel i Planas, 23
08034 Barcelona. Spain
T. 93 203 30 44
F. 93 204 65 34

Pere Cortacans

Folguerolas 46, 2°
08022 Barcelona. Spain
T. 93 211 78 62
F. 93 211 98 39

Pierre d'Avoine Architects

6A Orde Hall Street
London WC1N 3JW. United Kingdom
T. 171 242 21 24
F. 171 242 21 49

Rüdiger Lainer Architekt DI

Reisnerstrasse 41
A-1030 Wien. Austria
T. 43 1 713 37 06-0
F. 41 1 713 16 11 43

Thomas Hanrahan
Victoria Meyers Architects

22 West 21st Street
12th Floor
New York, NY 10010. U.S.A
T. 212 989 60 26
F. 212 255 37 76

Valerio Dewalt Train

200 North LaSalle Street
Chicago, Illinois 60601. U.S.A
T. 312 332 03 63
F. 312 332 47 27

Directory